AN INTRODUCTION TO

POTTERY

A STEP-BY-STEP PROJECT BOOK

CHARTWELL
BOOKS, INC.

A QUINTET BOOK

ISBN: 0-7858-0338-6

This book was designed and produced by
Quintet Publishing Limited
6, Blundell Street
London N7 9BH

Creative Director: Peter Bridgewater
Art Designer: Ian Hunt
Designer: Sally McKay
Project Editor: Sally Harper
Editor: Richard Rosenfeld
Jacket Design: Nik Morley

Typeset in Great Britain by
Central Southern Typesetters, Eastbourne
Manufactured in China by
Regent Publishing Services Limited.

This edition produced for sale in the USA,
its territories and dependencies only.

Published by Chartwell Books
A Division of Book Sales, Inc.
P.O. Box 7100

CONTENTS

Equipment

For the simplest clay shapes you need little equipment, just an absorbent cloth, a small wooden board, cutting wire and a small knife. If you want to economize use a wooden kitchen board and a cooking knife. A cut-up sheet will provide the cloth. Proper hand tools are essential. When buying tools always look for quality and effectiveness.

To begin with, work with clay in a fairly basic way to provide a chance to experience the material, feel how long it remains malleable, when it becomes dry, and when it starts to crack. Clay rewards careful handling, and does not like to be worked for too long – it can crumble to pieces.

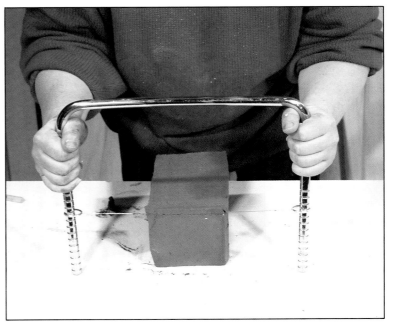

The work table should be stable, with a hard waterproof board. An oilcloth cover with a smooth surface is quite safe; the sharp fireclay edges, which can leave scratches on polished wood, will not cut this surface. In case this still seems too risky, work the clay on a board. Under the clay lay the cloth which prevents the clay from sticking to the surface. When you finish a piece place the finished work on a small board, preferably wooden. Again, place a cloth between the two surfaces, partly to soak up excess water.

First, however, cut the clay from the block with the wire. For shaping, smoothing and cutting, use the kitchen knife.

The next stage involves using a potter's wheel, enabling you to turn a piece and work on it from all sides. Accomplished handymen can even make their own wheels. Shops, however, offer a choice of wheels made from steel, cast steel, and aluminium; those with ball-bearings run smoothest. Wheels available for purchase have a diameter of 20–30cm (6.7–10in). You can buy wheels without a tripod which are placed on tables (table wheels) these are sufficient for school and home use. Their advantage is that after use they can be put away in a cupboard or on the shelf. Wheels with tripods are height-adjustable and stand free. Again, a cloth placed between the work and the wheel means you can detach the work more easily. For drying pieces of pottery use plaster boards, which soak up excess water. They are preferable to wooden boards.

ABOVE: **Showing the correct way to use the cutting wire on a piece of clay.**

LEFT: **Sieve and bowl, needed for sieving the glaze.**

After your initial attempts at pottery, it will be clear that tools besides your hands are necessary. A modelling tool has two differently-shaped ends. Depending on your needs, select a tool providing a long spoon and edges for a variety of purposes, from cutting to smoothing. Good modelling tools are made from wood, usually box or ebony. The harder the wood, the easier it is to work with. There are also simple plastic designs, but these soon become insufficient for your needs (for kindergartens and schools where high turnover must be reckoned with, these simple designs will suffice). Various pottery knives are also available, although a broad palette knife is best. Otherwise, a kitchen knife will suffice. However, modelling tools and mirettes are still very important. (You should purchase at least three mirettes and a variety of modelling tools.) That many are needed for shaping, removing clay from the work, and hollowing out thick pieces. Where modelling tools are too coarse, use sharper tools. With these you can carve out particularly delicate shapes, and carve your initials and the date of manufacture on the base. Alternative tools are knitting needles and toothpicks. If you want to make round holes for hanging pieces, or for patterns, try buying hole cutters. Alternatively, use an apple-corer. Forks are also extremely useful devices for roughening, engraving and scratching patterns. For smoothing and thickening use a beater, though always with the greatest care lest you knock a piece of pottery out of shape.

For shaping and preparing slabs of clay you need a clay roller. There are

BELOW: **You will need at least one knife; a kitchen knife is quite adequate. A cloth and wooden sticks for modelling are also important.**

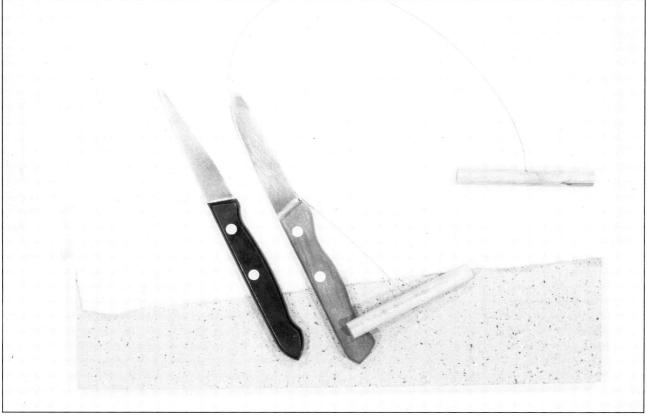

ABOVE: **A broad-handled cutting wire for carving out larger forms.**

BELOW: **You will need a mortar and pestle for grinding glazes.**

two kinds – a roller with ball-bearings (rolling pin), or a simple round stick with a diameter of about 35mm (1.4in). To create slabs of equal strength, work in two directions. And to obtain even, thick slabs, cut them with the cutting bow from the mass of clay.

When using the technique called turning, further aids are required, such as turning guides and sponges. Turning guides are similar to modelling tools, being made from hard wood, though some are plastic or metal; see which suits you best. Also necessary while turning are a small bucket of water and a sponge to soak up excess moisture. Natural sponges are preferable, being softer and more pliable than artificial sponges, but they are also more expensive. A sponge on a stick is useful for tall vessels.

Glazing aids

ABOVE: **Two types of rollers – choose either a rolling pin or a round stick.**

◆ · · ◆ · · · ◆ · · · ◆ · · · ◆ · · · ◆ · · · ◆ ·

A well glazed work is aesthetically pleasing; a badly glazed work can ruin an otherwise professionally made item. Here again, appropriate tools are the key to success. For glazing, various flat bristle brushes are available – but do not economize. Glazing brushes are 20–75mm (0.8–3in) wide. For most surfaces, a brush with a width of 25mm (1in) will suffice. Purchase a different brush for each glaze required to avoid rinsing after each session. When decorating finished pieces that have overglaze, middle glaze, and underglaze, you need fine to very fine animal-hair paintbrushes. Initially basic brushes will suffice, but for the best results you need

BELOW: **An engobing horn.**

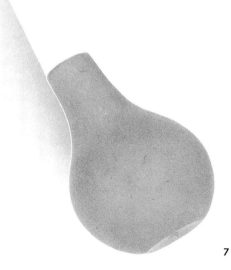

7

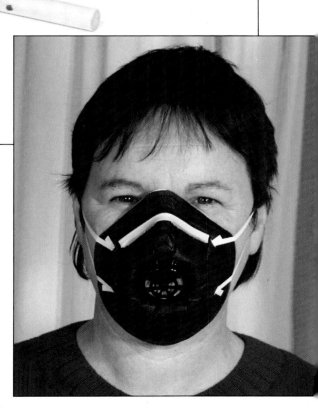

more expensive brushes. You can apply engobe with the engobing horn.

Initial attempts to apply the glaze can be made by spraying with a standard glaze spray. If however you wish to spray regularly, spraying equipment with an extractor unit must be purchased. In order to apply the glazes, use a glazing sieve. And finally, when mixing glazes, raw materials and engobes, always wear a dust mask to protect the mouth, since glazes contain unpleasant and often poisonous gases.

Molding with Clay

First steps

◆ · · · ◆ · · · ◆ · · · ◆ · · · ◆ · · · ◆ · · · ◆

The essential techniques for working clay are kneading and applying the slip. Kneading the clay is every bit as crucial as selecting the right type of clay. Before buying the clay it will have been through mixing machines and factory extruders. It is marketed in hanks and packaged in plastic covers. These packages of clay usually weigh either 10kg (22lb) or 25kg (55lb).

Although the clay has been well prepared, cleaned and mixed, it still requires kneading. The purpose of kneading is to spread the clay minerals, which are in the shape of small tiles, throughout the material, giving it a regular internal structure. Such kneading can only be carried out when the clay is first mixed with fireclay and water.

Kneading cannot be avoided. Its prime functions also include making the clay more plastic and malleable; it expels air bubbles, too, which will exist even in specially bought material. These air bubbles can have a devastating effect during firing. They expand at high temperatures and can easily shatter a piece if they cannot escape through the porous shard. Another potential problem can occur during wheel turning. Centrifugal force can propel air bubbles to the outside, ruining the pot's shape.

Before kneading, take a large piece of clay, weighing approximately 10kg (22lb). Place it on a steady table or hard surface. Place the cutting wire under the centre of the clay, and pull upwards, giving two pieces of equal size. Place one on top of the other and begin to knead. Next, turn the clay in a quarter circle to the left, and repeat the process. Again, use the wire to cut the clay

through the middle from below. Both lumps of clay are again kneaded one on top of the other, giving a piece with four layers. After the next operation there are eight layers, and by the time this has been done 20 times the clay is a well processed malleable mass.

There is another, slightly less arduous way of preparing the clay. This technique can however, only be used on small amounts. Cut a manageable 1–2kg (2.2–4.4lb) piece of clay from the lump, knead it on the table, and turn the clay in on itself like a snail-shell. It is important to work in only one direction, not forcing in any extra air bubbles.

1 Cutting the piece of clay in half with the cutting wire.

2 Two pieces of different-coloured clay ready for kneading.

3 Kneading, the clay by turning it in on itself.

4 After kneading, the clay is shaped into a smooth ball.

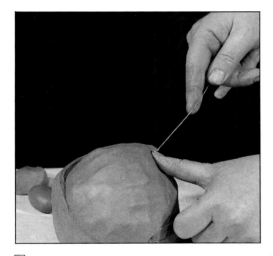

5 Cutting the correct sized piece of clay to be used.

6 Only work on as much clay as you think you will need for each piece.

Slip

◆ ··· ◆ ··· ◆ ··· ◆ ··· ◆ ··· ◆ ··· ◆

The slip is fine clay washed with a lot of water. Such sticky clay is required when attaching clay strips, creating tiles, or making repairs.

While you work the clay, you will find that small crumbs of clay result which dry very quickly. Collect them in a sealable jar and cover with water. After a couple of hours these dry remains will become a soft clay paste, or slip. Always keep the jar sealed for a ready supply. New crumbs can be added to it and again covered with water. To offset evaporation, top up with water from time to time. The slip should always have the consistency of paste, not liquid.

Clay slip can easily be combined with any work. The shaped pieces which are to be joined together are grazed with a fork, coated with slip, and joined together with gentle pressure. Slabs for joining together are cut with a rough edge – then apply plenty of slip to the joins and attach. For a really tight join insert a thin strip of clay into the connections. The slip penetrates the roughened and incised parts of the work and becomes inextricably linked with it. Any superfluous slip on the joins is left to dry and is removed with a scraper or knife. If it is removed too soon you run the risk of damaging the work irreparably.

Two pieces can never be joined together without a slip connection. Shortcuts never work and result in disasters during firing.

From clay to pottery

◆ ⋯ ◆ ⋯ ◆ ⋯ ◆ ⋯ ◆ ⋯ ◆ ⋯ ◆

The following procedure is standard. Practise it again and again until it is second nature. It is impossible to proceed without having mastered these stages.

1 Clay kneading (see explanation at the beginning of this chapter).

2 Removing the required amount of clay and shaping it into a ball.

3 Forming the piece.

4 If decorations are to be applied, do this now. Provided the clay is still soft you can incise, stamp, impress, and attach pieces to it.

5 Hollowing out – if a piece is more than 2cm (0.8in) thick, it must be hollowed out to remove trapped air bubbles. For hollowing out, slice the piece in two with the cutting wire. Before cutting, remember to mark a spot on the cutting line so that the pieces can be fitted exactly together.

The clay is carefully hollowed out from the inside with a scraper. The thickness of the remaining wall is approximately 4–10mm (0.16–0.4in) according to the piece. Stick it back together with slip and make a small open-

ABOVE: **Slipware cockerel dish by William Newland, UK. The white slip was applied to the red body and the design then trailed with a warm, dark clay.**

BELOW: **A porcelain incised dish by Ann Clark, UK. The design was incised into the clay body at the leather-hard stage. When biscuited, it was glazed with a transparent glaze then fired to 2,340°F (1,280°C).**

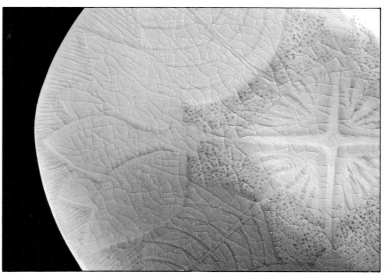

RIGHT: **Showing how pigments react with glazes. Six basic colouring oxides were added to a standard transparent alkaline glaze and a standard transparent lead-based glaze.**

ing so that the expanding air can escape.

6 Now is the time to paint the work. Do it when the clay has become leather-hard.

7 Carefully place the work on a shelf to dry. The clay becomes brittle, and dries out, so special care is necessary. From now on handle any item with both hands. Never attempt to lift the work by its attached parts or handle. These parts are extremely delicate and break off immediately. Damage to pieces which are already dry are almost beyond repair. (The drying process is described in detail on page 20.)

8 Biscuit firing. Once the pieces are well dried, they are carefully placed in the kiln and exposed to the fire. After the kiln has cooled down, remove the pieces. Although they are no longer as delicate as before firing, do not pick them up by pieces which could easily break off. Methods of firing and placing pieces in the kiln are described in detail in chapter 9.

9 The work is glazed and painted. You will learn more about these techniques in chapter 8.

10 Glost firing. After this stage the finished pieces can be removed from the kiln. If drops of glaze are hanging on the base, sand them on the grinding wheel or with sandpaper. Care must be taken because splinters of glaze are sharp.

Iron oxide gives a reddish brown reaction in a strong lead based glaze

Manganese oxide gives a purple reaction in an alkaline based glaze.

Copper oxide will give a sharper green when used in a lead based glaze.

Cobalt oxide is little affected by the type of glaze.

Pottery without a Wheel

Hand building and pinch pots

Having mastered the introductory stages, it is time to discuss the basic 'creative' techniques. The first, for making a small dish, merely involves squeezing and shaping the ball of clay. This pinching technique requires only your hands and a cutting wire for removing the clay. Use standard, semi-plastic clay. For decorating you will also need a brush. Since you are using only your hands, you can work quickly. As the hands become warm they quickly dry the clay, making it crack. It is therefore advisable to have a slightly damp sponge on the table to wet your hands.

1 From the kneaded clay, cut a fist-sized piece and shape it into a ball.

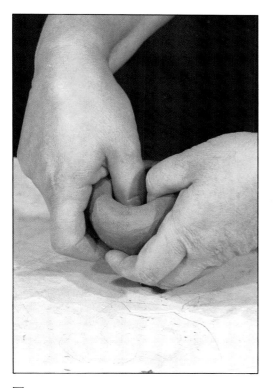

2 With the thumb of one hand make a depression in the clay while pressing lightly against the inside with the other hand. Rotate the ball at the same time.

3 The walls become thinner and are pushed upwards. Take care to work from bottom to top; if you work the edge first, it cracks and becomes limp.

4 To form the edge, run lightly over it with your fingertips. With one hand keep the edge in shape and with the other, carefully smooth it.

5 The outside surface of the pot is smoothed with a modelling stick.

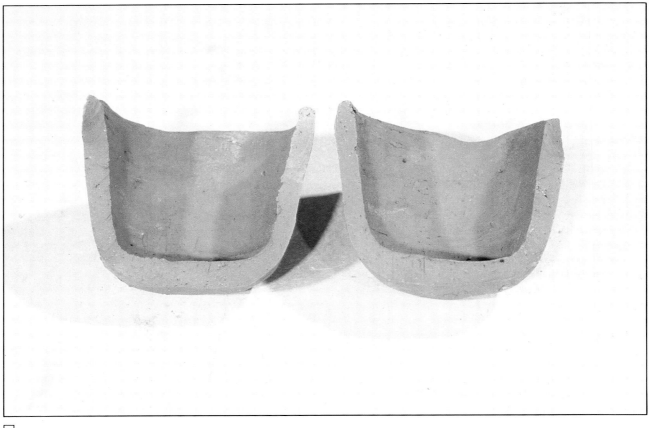

6 A cross-section showing the finished form of your pinch pot.

Hand flatterer

◆ · · · ◆ · · · ◆ · · · ◆ · · · ◆ · · · ◆ · · · ◆ ·

For the second piece of work, a hand flatterer, again you need only use your hands. This time, however, use clay containing fine fireclay. Take a piece large enough to fit inside the hand. Squeeze the clay into shape, letting it follow the shape of your hand. Next, let it dry, polish it with your palms and fingertips, and place it to dry on the shelf next to the dishes. If the dish was a rather useful object, the hand flatterer is certainly not. It has aesthetic rather than practical value.

Small figurative animals

· ◆ · · · ◆ · · · ◆ · · · ◆ · · · ◆ · · · ◆ · · · ◆ ·

The third piece of work is a small animal figure. To make it you will require a kneaded semi-plastic clay and scratching and modelling tools. These small figurative works are great fun, much liked by children.

ABOVE: **To make a beetle, cut the oval lump of clay through the middle. Carve the head, eyes and wings, then paint on spots of slip in a contrasting colour. Place on a shelf to dry.**

LEFT: **Little animals are made from small pieces of clay formed in oval shapes.**

15

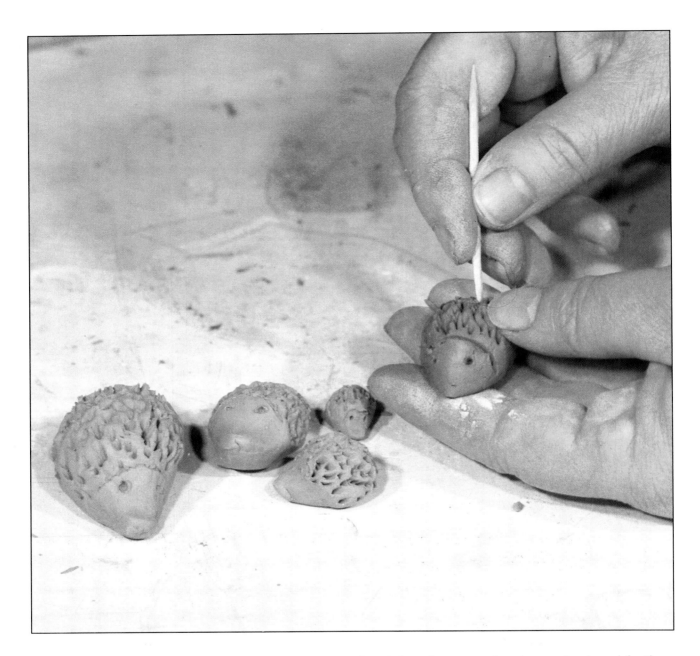

ABOVE: **For a small hedgehog, squeeze a little nose. The spines are created by piercing the clay with scissors. Alternatively, make them separately and attach with slip. The eyes and mouth are carved in.**

For the small *bird* you will need slightly more time. The head comes from a second, slightly smaller oval ball of clay. Attach this with slip to the other piece, to form the bird's body. Now, squeeze the beak out of the lump (a separate beak would break off too easily). Likewise, shape the tail from the lump. However, you can form the feathers and wings from small coils of clay. All the features – head, eyes, beak and feathers – can be applied by 'scratching' them on. If you have made a large bird with ruffled feathers, pierce it repeatedly from below. This is important so that possible trapped air bubbles do not destroy the work during firing. Using the techniques described, it is possible to create a wide range of animals, and more fantastic creatures.

Jar and lid

❖ ⋯ ❖ ⋯ ❖ ⋯ ❖ ⋯ ❖ ⋯ ❖ ⋯ ❖

The fourth piece of work is a small jar with lid to contain coins, jewellery, and small utensils. The material to be used is once again semi-plastic kneaded clay, and the tools are cutting wire, a mirette, and various modelling sticks.

1 With the cutting wire remove enough clay to form a ball about 7–10 cm (2.7– 4 in) in diameter. Work the ball of clay until well rounded; smooth with a teaspoon.

2 Now place the cutting wire in the upper half – hold in at one end and pull through until you have almost split the clay in two. By moving the wire down a little a 'nose' is created.

17

3 The ball is then split into two pieces which fit on top of each other.

4 Take the mirette and slowly start to hollow out the ball with circular motions.

5 Continue the process until the half-ball has a uniformly thick wall, no wider than a little finger.

6 Repeat the process with the other half-ball of clay.

7 Smooth the inner walls with a finger tip.

8 With care, you will find that the two halves will fit exactly on top of each other. Now even the base.

9 To create a small knob for the lid, use a fork to roughen the spot on the lid where the knob will be placed. Do the same to the underside of the ball.

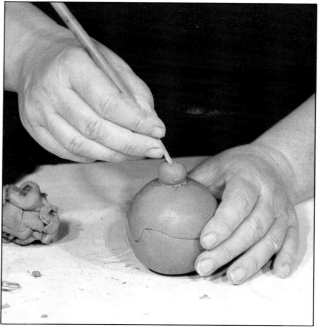

10 Coat both roughened spots with slip and attach the knob. Place the jar on a shelf to dry; insert a sheet of tissue between jar and lid so they don't stick together.

The Coiling Technique

This technique is probably the most frequently used method when making clay vessels without a potter's wheel. Coils of clay are placed on top of one another. Shapes made from a ball of clay, like a dish, can only be made up to a certain size, after which success becomes difficult, if not impossible. Also, a shape which tapers towards the top, or a closed vessel, are ruled out by this method. However, coiling permits complex structures, and without restriction on size.

Vase or beaker

◆ · · · ◆ · · · ◆ · · · ◆ · · · ◆ · · · ◆ · · · ◆ ·

The first piece of work in this new technique is a vessel (used as a vase, or, if made small, a beaker). The following tools are required: small board or a banding wheel as a base, over which a cloth is placed; modelling tools; small knife for smoothing; and cutting wire. Slip is not normally used with the coiling method as it makes the clay too damp and slippery.

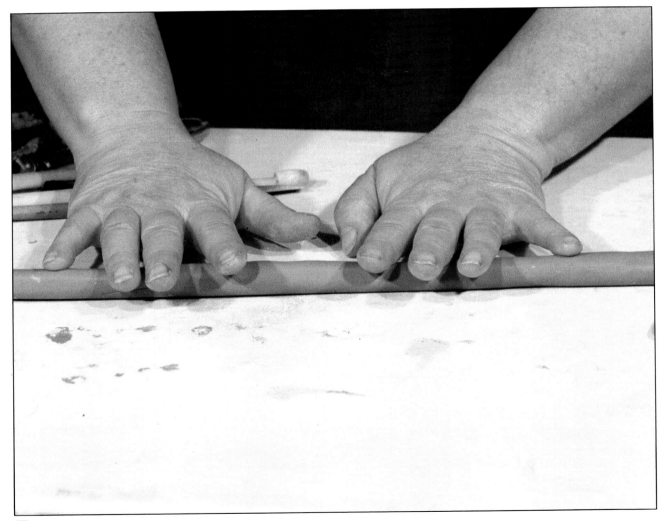

1 Slice off a piece of clay with the cutting wire and roll it into a coil the thickness of a thumb. This provides the base of the vessel and is coiled into a spiral.

2 Do not make the diameter too large, or you will end up with a vessel that is far too big. It is best to take an existing vessel of the right size and use it as a guide.

3 With the knife smooth the base from top to bottom, where necessary cutting it to provide a round shape. A pair of dividers will help establish the shape. More coils are rolled out, up to four or five in total. The first coil is placed on the edge of the base and attached.

21

4 The first and following coils must be 'welded' to achieve an even shape. If you proceed upwards in one long coil the work loses its shape.

5 Note that you must weld the base and coil inside and outside. Carefully smooth the clay in a downward direction with a modelling tool or your thumb. Once the coil is fixed in position, clean the join in a lateral direction. Put the second coil in place, taking care that the subsequent coil finishes in a different position.

6 & 7 **Carefully smooth the work, first inside then outside.**

8 As the number of coils increases, it becomes possible to lift the vessel without danger of ruining its shape. From now on the pace of work can increase.

9 Three coils are put in place. All three coils are then smoothed in the same way as before, both inside and outside. Now clean them and continue building to the desired height.

10 & 11 Squeeze the upper edge between thumb and forefinger to make it thinner, whilst smoothing it delicately with the fingertips of the other hand.

If you want to make a vase with a bulbous form, proceed in the following way. At the height where the vase is to become bulbous, place the coils further outwards rather than directly on top of each other. (Be careful: due to pressure whilst smoothing the outside, the clay easily moves out. Hold it in shape with the other hand.) If you now wish to narrow the vessel, attach the coils on the inside and add each coil separately. In this way you can, with some practice, make a spherical vase with a narrow opening.

Slab Building

Slabs of clay can be made in two different ways: by rolling it out with a clay roller, or by cutting it from a large lump with the aid of a cutting wire. The latter is particularly suitable when you need several slabs of the same length. The clay should form a mass of slabs beaten into a block. The lengths of the sides must have the dimensions of the final slabs. Cut off slabs of equal thickness with the slab cutter.

If you require slabs of varying size, roll out the clay on the cloth, using the roller. If you roll on two battens you obtain a slab of even thickness, from which any shape can be cut. This method of slab building is less strenuous than the other method, but does have disadvantages. It is not only more difficult to make several slabs of the same size (the clay easily goes out of shape during cutting and removal), but rolled out slabs buckle more quickly than cut slabs.

Nameplate

◆ ··· ◆ ··· ◆ ··· ◆ ··· ◆ ··· ◆ ··· ◆ ·

Use this new technique to create a nameplate, bearing either your name, or that of the person receiving the gift. Think about the design, and the extent of decoration and imagery. For the sake of this example, we will use the name W. Bumble, who lives in London.

The following equipment is required: roller; two battens of equal thickness; a new cloth; modelling tools; and a hole piercer. Use semi-plastic well-kneaded clay. Since white paint will be used, select white clay, and white slip.

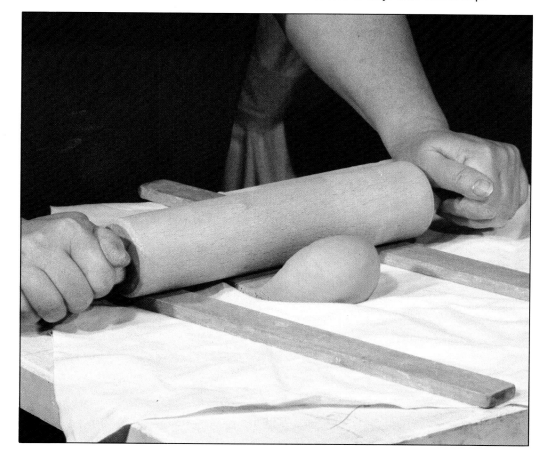

1 **Cut off a piece of kneaded clay and shape it into a ball. Roll the clay out on the cloth between the wooden battens, which serve as a support. Occasionally turn the clay, which becomes progressively easy to work. The cloth absorbs any excess moisture, and can be washed, dried and reused. Next, place the rolled clay on the plaster board or a firm surface covered in newspaper to dry. Since paper and plaster are absorbent, the clay slab becomes more solid and does not lose its shape so quickly.** 27

2 Next, cut a template out of paper. If the finished plate is to have specific dimensions, take into account shrinkage during drying and firing. Use the template to cut the shape out of the clay slab. Place this on the cloth. Meanwhile, the remaining clay is mixed together and briefly kneaded. Store it in a plastic cover so that it can be used again. Extra decorative pieces can be mounted with slip, though carved motifs are easier to make.

3 Apply the name using clay coils; mark it on the slab and then remove. Carve into the marked places, taking care not to apply too much slip afterwards.

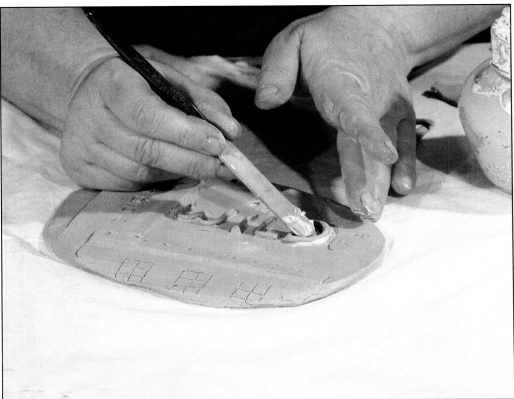

4 The name is fixed in place with light pressure. Carefully wipe and smooth away excess slip. If you want to paint the plate, study chapter 8, 'Forming the Surface'. Engobing (painting with earth colours) must be done now, while the clay is still damp.

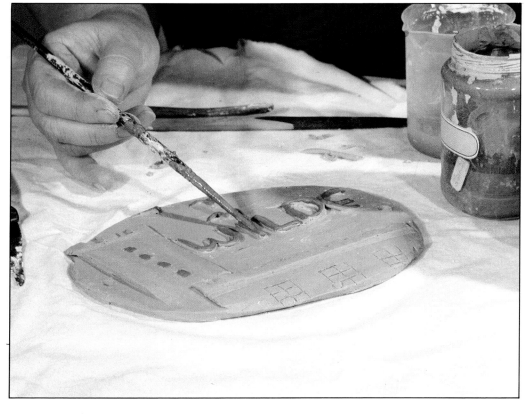

5 Do not forget the holes for screwing in the plate. When making these holes, cut right through the plate and clean the edges. As a test, stick a screw through (take shrinkage into account). If using two holes, align them carefully. Finally, the work is dried on a plaster board or board covered with newspaper. To prevent the slab from warping whilst drying, cover with a cloth.

Relief work

◆ · · · ◆ · · · ◆ · · · ◆ · · · ◆ · · · ◆ · · · ◆ ·

The contrast between light and shadow, colour and black and white, and shiny and matt surfaces is very important. It creates tension which can be the subject of a specific item.

If you want to create a large relief work, big enough to cover a wall, it is advisable to make this out of small individual slabs, and to assemble them on a board after firing. Slabs which are too large suffer tensions during drying and firing, and easily crack. For this example we will choose a regular hexagon as the basic shape. Its advantage is that one piece can be added to another in a honeycombed shape, which can be extended and enlarged at will. Try out various techniques on the different parts for an amusing effect. The honeycomb piece is ideal for group work.

The following equipment is required: a roller; two wooden battens approximately 75cm (29in) thick; knife; slip; modelling tools; fork; and an assortment of shapes for stamping, such as screws, snail-shells, buttons, leaves, rings, indeed anything which leaves an imprint.

Up to a diameter of 15cm (5in) you can work in semi-plastic clay, but if you are starting with larger slabs, the fire-clay content must be higher. For this purpose, specialist shops offer 'slab clay'. The hexagon shape is not compulsory; a square is a reasonable alternative.

1 Cut a template of the basic shape. A hexagon is constructed as follows: with dividers make a circle and mark the radius at six points, then join these points together.

2 From the clay rolled out to a thickness of approximately 7–8mm (0.3in) cut 3–4 slabs.

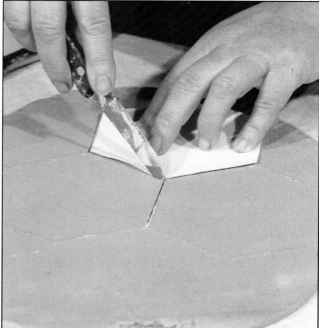

3 The slabs are not worked on immediately, but packed airtight and put to one side for later use.

4 Smooth and trim all edges carefully.

5 On the slab to be worked, lightly mark a pattern. With screws, buttons, modelling tools or other objects the various motifs are imprinted.

6 With the next slab proceed differently, applying the motifs using strips, balls and spirals.

7 On the slab base, draw the pattern; carve along the drawn lines and apply slip, and with light pressure attach the pieces.

8 If the slabs are to be hung together, it is better if the patterns match.

9 On the third slab attach a tree shape.

10 Make the trunk from half a clay coil and press it on both sides into the slab with a modelling tool (do not forget to carve in and apply slip).

11 The top of the tree consists of single leaves – begin from the outside and work inwards. Attach the top in one piece and then add single branches with leaves.

12 An apple tree looks very good, particularly with apples amid the boughs and leaves.

33

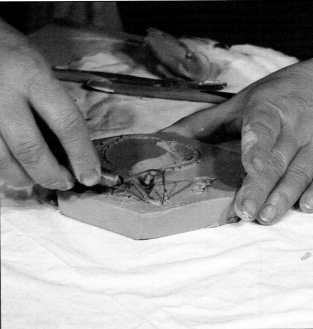

13 The classical method of making a relief is by hollowing clay out of the slab. To do this take a thick slab so that it can be hollowed out up to 5–8mm (0.25in).

14 Sketch the motif and cut it out with the mirette. The clay is then smoothed out with modelling tools.

15 With the hexagon you can continue making pieces endlessly. For hanging, holes must be pierced.

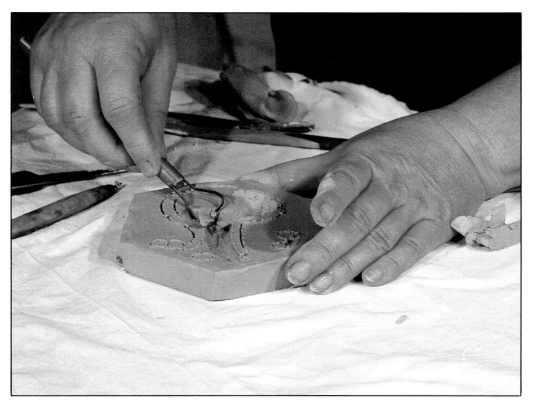

RIGHT: **If you want to mount the slabs on a board, make hollows in the back where adhesive will form. Drill holes in the wooden board or chipboard, so the adhesive can also stick here.**

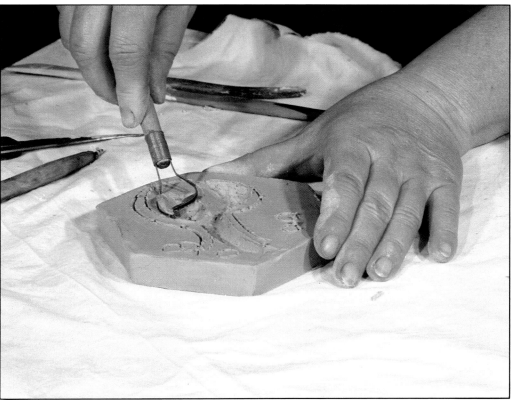

Throwing and the Wheel

Working on the potter's wheel is a totally new experience and demands great patience and practice. Although it looks easy to master, it can take many hours before you produce the shapes you require. Note that an absolute must for throwing on the wheel is well-kneaded clay, free of air bubbles. Water is also used, though applied in a different way from 'hand building'. The hands are always kept damp, and a bucket of water must therefore be kept near the wheel. A sponge is also crucial to absorb excess water.

The following equipment is required: cutting wire; needle; mirette; sharp knife; a turning guide; and, of course, water and sponge.

Centring

[1] Use well-kneaded throwing clay to shape a ball, about 1 kg (2.2lb) in weight. Throw this ball as near as possible to the middle of the wheel, which is turning in an anti-clockwise direction.

[2] Grasp the clay firmly, push it onto the wheel, and squeeze. By doing this the clay changes its shape and moves slightly upwards. Now hold the clay firmly with your left hand and press down with the right, immediately letting it move upwards again. Using the base of both palms the clay is pressed conically upwards.

[3] Repeat this process several times, until the clay runs smoothly between your hands and has stopped wobbling. While doing this, beware of any jerky movements, with hands or with the wheel. The clay is extremely plastic and reacts to any movement, instantly losing its shape. To get a safe hold, press both upper arms tight against your body.

36

Opening up

◆ · · · ◆ · · · ◆ · · · ◆ · · · ◆ · · · ◆ · · · ◆ ·

Before opening up, the lump of spinning clay should be dome-shaped. With both thumbs press a hole in the middle, enlarging it with your left hand. If your hands are touching during this process, you can control them better. Work them down into the clay until you have reached the base. Take care while doing this, because you must be left with a base that is not too thin. If it is, it will break or distort on being removed from the wheel. Slowly stop the wheel to test the thickness of the base with a needle. If satisfied, set the wheel in motion again. If the base is too thin, it is best to start again from the beginning, since it is practically impossible to correct this problem. When the clay is spinning, pull it slowly outwards with the left hand to the desired diameter. With your thumbs in the opening, run both hands over the clay once more, and gently press the mass inwards again.

Lifting

❖ ··· ❖ ··· ❖ ··· ❖ ··· ❖ ··· ❖ ··· ❖ .

Move your left hand into the clay to maintain the shape. With your right hand, or better with the knuckle of the index finger, carefully raise the height of the clay. Be careful, however, not to make the sides too thin. Repeat this process several times with smooth, flowing movements, to create a cylinder with walls of equal thickness. Whilst working, continually dampen your hands to lubricate the clay and prevent it from sticking to your fingers. If the clay should become dry, friction results and the piece loses its shape. As soon as the walls threaten to become too thin, draw the thumb and index finger of the left hand over them. In this way, the superfluous clay is removed and the walls will thicken.

Should you be unlucky enough to discover an air bubble, pierce the work with a needle. In bad cases, this may necessitate a fresh start.

❖ ··· ❖ ··· ❖ ··· ❖ ··· ❖ ··· ❖ ··· ❖ ··· ❖ ··· ❖ ··· ❖ ··· ❖ ··· ❖ ··· ❖

1 Gradually the piece takes its form from the guidance of your left hand.

2 Be careful not to let the walls become too thin.

3 A bulbous shape is made by squeezing out a bulge in the cylinder from base to top.

Shaping

The easiest object to create is a *bowl*, since on the wheel the clay is automatically pushed outwards by centrifugal force. Ensure, however, that you always work from the bottom to the top, and never the reverse. Also check that your left hand shapes while the right gives constant counterpressure.

If the walls of the bowl widen too quickly they will begin to wobble and tear. Also take care that individual areas do not widen too far, or the walls will collapse because the clay above the weak points becomes too heavy.

RIGHT: **Putting the finishing touches to a bulbous bowl. Using the three basic techniques — cylinder, opening up and throwing inwards — you can create any conceivable shape.**

ABOVE: **If you want to narrow the shape at the top, grasp the cylinder with both hands and push the clay upwards applying gentle pressure. Not only will the diameter slowly decrease, but the walls will thicken automatically. Place the left hand inside, while the right presses lightly against it from outside to make the walls thinner.**

LEFT: **If you want to make a bulbous shape, first make the basic cylinder – narrow it at the top and proceed using your left hand by squeezing out the bulge from the bottom to the top. The right hand lightly guides the shape from the outside. To make a *jug* with a neck, create pressure with the right hand outside, guide the clay inwards, and throw a straight cylinder from the remaining clay to form the neck.**

41

Handle

◆ ∙ ∙ ∙ ◆ ∙ ∙ ∙ ◆ ∙ ∙ ∙ ◆ ∙ ∙ ∙ ◆ ∙ ∙ ∙ ◆ ∙ ∙ ∙ ◆ ∙

If there is another part to be added to the thrown shape, such as a handle, attach it after turning off. Handles can be made in various ways. The simplest is to roll out a clay coil and attach this as a handle. Yet this has a disadvantage since stretching the clay, when bending it, causes cracks to form easily, making the handle fragile. Moreover, a flat handle looks better than a thick one.

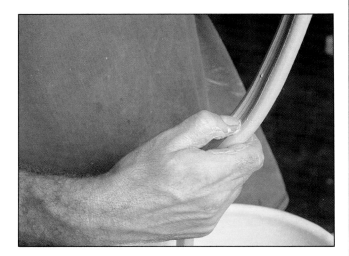

[1] Stretch and smooth a clay coil to form a flat handle.

[2] Mark the areas where the handle will be attached, then

tease both places.

3 A conically shaped clay coil is placed on the work table, and is stretched and smoothed at the same time using water. Then cut the now flat strip of clay from the surface, hold it with your left hand, smooth it and pull it into the desired shape under running water with your right hand. Rinse your hands at the same time. Hang the strip of clay, now recognizable as a handle, over your right hand, and press the upper end onto the marked position.

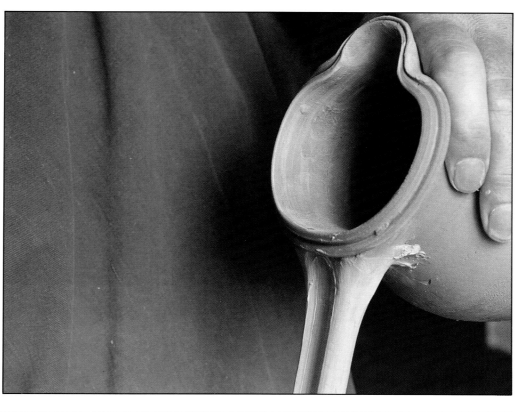

4 Press the lower end with your thumb into its place, squeezing off the surplus part of the strip. Clean the joints with a sponge or modelling tool. If you are not quite sure whether the handle will hold, use a small coil of clay to help. When attaching and smoothing the handle, its shape must not be damaged. Also take care that it does not lie above the rim of the vessel.

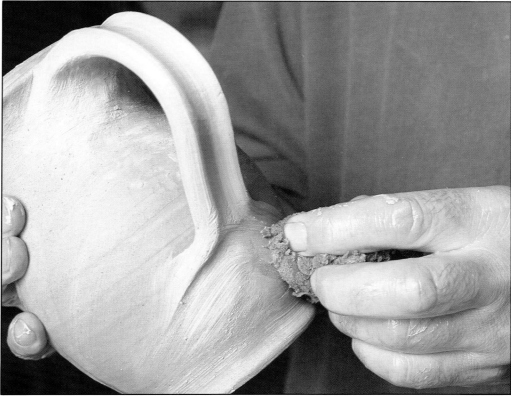

Firing

Biscuit firing

◆ · · · ◆ · · · ◆ · · · ◆ · · · ◆ · · · ◆ · · · ◆ ·

Clay obtains its strength through firing, with malleable clay being transformed into a solid ceramic. In the heat of the fire the clay sinters, which means that its minerals fuse and solidify.

Two firings are necessary in order to make ceramics covered with glaze, from the greenware. With biscuit firing, the ware is prepared for glazing, although theoretically a first firing is not necessary. Some manufacturers avoid this, believing that the glaze penetrates unfired glazed clay more effectively. For domestic purposes, however, it is easier to work on the clay after biscuit firing, since the unfired ware is very fragile and easily broken.

Biscuit fire at 900°C (1,382°F). At this temperature the clay is solid, but still sufficiently porous for the glaze to adhere. The final temperatures should be arrived at gradually, since chemical transformations take place during firing. The first critical phase is at 200°–300°C (392°–572°F), the second at about 600°C (1,112°F). There are particles in the clay which begin to vitrify at these temperatures, and stick the substances together. Since these chemical reactions put a strain on the work, these should be approached slowly.

BELOW: **Showing the use of tongs to move pots in the kiln.**

TEMPERATURE ADJUSTMENT AND FIRING

A wide variety of electronically controlled kilns, in which you only need set a program are now available. There are at least two programs, one for biscuit firing and the other for glaze firing. There are, additionally, manufacturers who offer programs which can operate more complex firing cycles. Such kilns have very reliable temperature controls, and a sensor measuring the degree of heat in the kiln.

In less sophisticated kilns, which have no electronic controls, the temperature is measured with pyrometric cones (three-sided thin pyramids). They are made in such a way that they will melt and bend at a given temperature. Three cones are placed in an observation window in the kiln, where they can easily be seen. The middle cone is linked to the temperature required for firing and begins to lose its shape when the desired temperature is reached. The cone before it is for a lower temperature, and will by this stage have already fallen. The third cone will fall at a higher temperature. These cones are obtainable in grades from 600° to 2,000°C (1,112° to 3,632°F).

Electronic kilns, in which it is only necessary to select and set a program, are extremely expensive. However, there

BELOW: **Glazing a piece after the initial biscuit firing.**

45

are kilns in which temperature, heat output, and holding time of the temperature reached must be set at the beginning of the firing. They automatically control the temperature and will switch off at the required moment.

For the first firing phase up to 300°C (572°F) you need a heat output of only 20–30 per cent. At this most critical stage the remaining water is also expelled from the work. If there is still too much moisture in the work, unable to escape, there will be an explosion in the kiln. The second firing phase, up to approximately 600°C (1,112°F), is reached with about 50–60 per cent heat output. Often there is a time switch built in for this second firing stage. Select from four to six hours for sensitive and thick pieces of work, and two to four hours for other, more basic pieces. The third firing phase, up to 900°C (1,652°F) can be achieved with the full output of the kiln. The pieces are already solid, and all moisture will have evaporated. This temperature is held for about 20 minutes. Since electronic kilns control and regulate these firing stages automatically, they are obviously an asset. If possible, try to use one.

Packing the kiln

· ◆ · · · ◆ · · · ◆ · · · ◆ · · · ◆ · · · ◆ · · · ◆ ·

To make the best possible use of space in the kiln, you will need to add shelves. These can be made from refractory tiles and kiln props, tiles being available in a range of sizes. For intermediate layers which do not take up the entire base of the kiln, use one or two half-tiles. It is also possible to use tiles with holes, which heat more rapidly since they have less mass, and therefore use up less electricity. However, these tiles have two disadvantages: they are fragile and break easily; and if, during glaze firing, the works are too thickly glazed, the substance can drip on to items situated below.

For plates and tiles, shelves are available on which they can be placed to save space. Since in biscuit firing glazes do not melt and the pieces cannot stick together, smaller items can be placed inside larger ones. Extreme caution is advised, however, when doing this, because the pieces are easily broken. Do not carry pieces by their handles, but lift and support them. Also, avoid placing heavy pieces on top of thin, light, fragile pieces. Never try to cram too many small items inside a larger one, and remember that openings can shrink during firing. It is very tempting to place flat tiles inside other pieces, since they are particularly difficult to pack. But they are also among the most sensitive pieces at this firing stage. Such tiles are best placed flat in such a way that they will take up little room.

It is very important that there is good air circulation within the kiln. The best place, therefore, for flat pieces is in the middle of the kiln. Round pieces usually survive firing without any problems, and can be placed anywhere. You should also try to place pieces of similar height together. Small pieces are situated on the lowest level, with kiln props. They must reach at least 3–4mm (¹⁄₁₀in) above the highest piece of work, so that the heavy fire clay bat does not crush the greenware. This can easily be checked with a wooden batten, moving from one prop to another.

If you build on three props, the bat resting on them cannot wobble since it will be well supported. The props are arranged in a triangle, and should as far